This book is dedicated to children and families
who don't look the same, but love the same.

A note from the author:

Welcome to the world of SweetPea. SweetPea is all races and genders, known only by the design of the fabric worn exclusively by this character. SweetPea's parents are likewise known by the design of their clothing. They may be a bi-racial same-gender couple on one page, and on the next, a samerace mix-gendered couple. Similarly, on one page, SweetPea maybe an Afro-American girl, and the next, a Native American boy, while on the following page, SweetPea may be a gender-neutral Anglo-American child.

This book is intended to honor diversity in the human experience. Written in epicene (gender-neutral) terms, it utilizes the Shakespearian use of pronouns – their, theirs, them, themselves – as singular pronouns, with nongender binary usage of the word "their" to represent a single individual. Whether in terms of race, gender, sexual orientation, or religion, we are one people upon one Earth, and this is a fact worth celebrating. It is my sincere desire that you enjoy the adventures of SweetPea as much as I have enjoyed writing them.

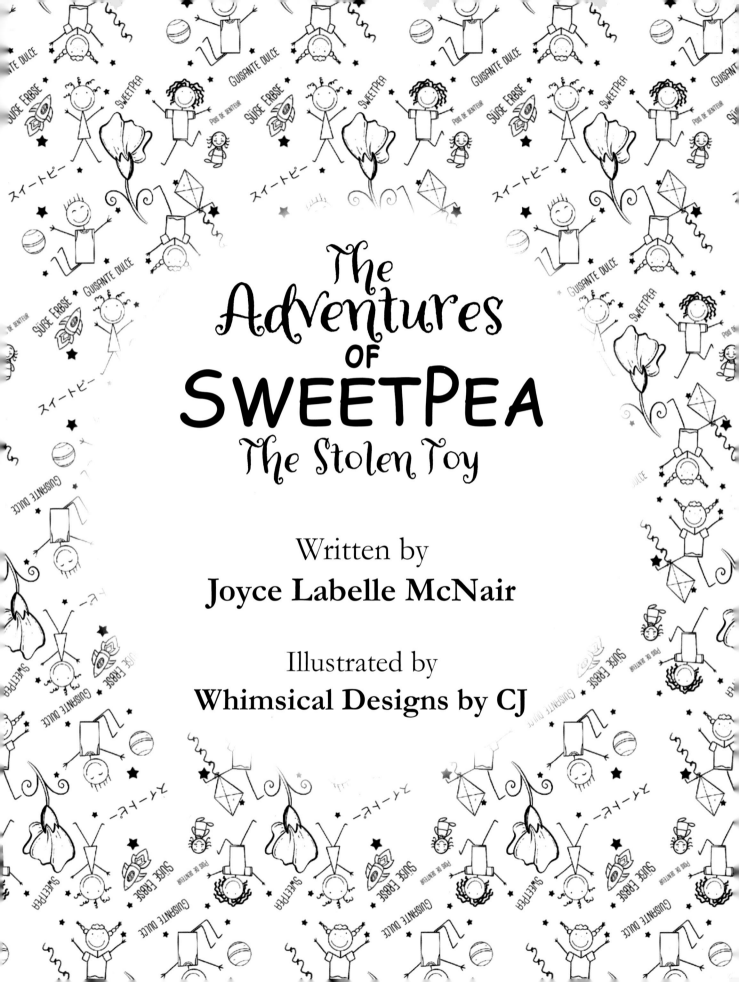

The Adventures OF SweetPea
The Stolen Toy

Written by
Joyce Labelle McNair

Illustrated by
Whimsical Designs by CJ

SweetPea's parents woke them up early. It was the day they had all planned to go to the bookstore. Dada and Papa took them twice a month to the bookstore for storytelling with Yami.

SweetPea loved to hear how, when reading stories, Yami's voice would rise and fall. His eyes, arms, and feet all helped to tell the stories that he read. Yami funny faces always made SweetPea laugh. SweetPea was filled with amazement as he read stories of fishing trips, rocket flights to the moon, and treasure maps.

"SweetPea, breakfast is ready," Mama called.

"Let me brush my teeth and I'm on my way, Mama."

"Here you go, your favorite breakfast, pancakes and bacon. Now, today is going to be a short trip to the bookstore. We have to leave as soon as the storyteller is finished," Mama said.

"What time does the bookstore open? Is Yami going to be reading today? Are we still going?" SweetPea asked.

"Calm down, SweetPea, eat your food. Yes, we are going to the bookstore today and yes, Yami will be there reading. The bookstore opens at 9:30, so we'll be there in time to listen to Yami read," Papa said.

The day was not too hot – a beautiful sunny spring day with clear skies. The family hopped in the car, fastened their seatbelts, and began the drive to the bookstore, only a short distance from SweetPea's home.

When they arrived, Momma reminded SweetPea that they were only going to listen to Yami's story and then leave, because Papa had to go home after that and work on a project.

"What? No books? No toy? But I've been good all week, I thought I was going to get a reward!" SweetPea exclaimed.

"No, not today, SweetPea. We don't give you a reward every time you're good or do your chores. Papa and I want you to try every day to make good choices, and giving you a reward every time wouldn't be the best thing to help you do that. Rewards are optional," Momma explained.

SweetPea gave a long sigh and held back their tears.

"Just think of the fun you'll
have listening to Yami,"
Papa encouraged.

SweetPea felt a little better and smiled a little, but inside, they were hurt
because they had been thinking about getting a new toy
and listening to Yami.

They'd hoped that today would be the day their parents would buy a new toy to add to their growing collection.

Soon, the family arrived at the bookstore.

"Yami!" called SweetPea, running up to their friend.

"It's so good to see you, SweetPea," he greeted.

"Can I help you get ready?" SweetPea asked.

"Sure you can, I can always use some help. Thank you for asking,"
Yami said.

"What story are you reading today?" Is it an old story or something new?
I can't wait to hear it, I'm so excited!" exclaimed SweetPea.

Yami chose a series of poems from one of SweetPea's favorite books.

Children began to gather in the reading room of the bookstore, many of their faces familiar to SweetPea.

There were Josh, Jake, Courtney, Shannon, and Alex. Soon, the room was full of eager faces, all waiting for him to begin reading.

SweetPea sat and listened in delight.

Their minds wandered and daydreamed as Yami
read the poems that were so dear to them.

Yami's voice rose and fell.
His arms swayed like branches
in the wind.

Yami beat a drum as he read,
and the harmonic meter of
the poems kept the children
mesmerized as they sat and
listened intently.

All too soon, Yami's reading time was over. But SweetPea wasn't ready for the reading to finish. Nor were they ready to leave the bookstore.

Aww, not now, please please please, just one more!"

Yami smiled.
"Next time, SweetPea. Our time is finished for today, and we need to respect the next person who's scheduled to use this room."

SweetPea became angry and frustrated that he couldn't continue.
They wanted to hear him read more poems.

Papa reached for SweetPea's hand, saying it was time to leave.
"Thank Yami for reading to you today, SweetPea."

SweetPea pouted and refused to take Papa's hand. "It's not fair!
I don't want to leave the bookstore!"

SweetPea stomped their foot. "Why did Papa come with us? Papa could have stayed home and now I have to leave! Now I can't stay and play with my friends! I don't want to go!" SweetPea shouted.

Momma's face became stern. Reaching for SweetPea's hand, Momma said, "Would you like to stay home the next time Yami reads at the bookstore?
Or are you going to take my hand so we can leave?"

"No, Momma, no!" SweetPea cried.

"Then let's go, Papa needs to be home soon."

SweetPea was so angry that they ran off,
telling Momma they had to go to the bathroom.

But instead of going there, SweetPea snuck into the toy section. They grabbed the toy they had been wanting and stuck it in their pocket.

Then, SweetPea ran back to Momma, full of smiles. Momma wondered about the sudden change in mood, but was in a hurry to get home and forgot to ask SweetPea about it.

As soon as they got home, SweetPea ran upstairs to play with their new toy in secret. Papa wanted to talk to them about SweetPea yelling in the bookstore, but also needed to finish a project for work before SweetPea's attitude could be addressed.

SweetPea was in their bedroom,
playing with the stolen toy.
They were having so much fun that
they didn't notice Papa peeping
through the door, watching them
play with the stolen toy.

"Where did you get this?"
Papa asked, pointing at the stolen toy.

"I-I-I," SweetPea stammered.

Papa asked again. "Where did you get this toy?"

"Please, Papa, I wanted to stay, I wanted a toy. I've been very good —
I brushed my teeth, I made my bed, I did my chores. I fed Rex and I
took the trash out for Momma," SweetPea pleaded.

"Answer my question, SweetPea," Papa said seriously.

"I took it, I took it!" cried SweetPea.

"No, you did not take that toy, you stole that toy. I am very disappointed in you. Shame on you for stealing. Mama and I have taught you better than to steal from others. I know exactly what I'm going to do, and it will make you think twice before you steal again. Get your coat. We're going back to the bookstore to return that toy to Ms. Boatwright, the bookstore owner. She will get to decide whether to call the police."

"No, Papa, no, I can't face her! I'm scared!"
SweetPea cried.

"Get your coat at once, and don't say another word until you say it to
Ms. Boatwright," Papa said angrily.

SweetPea burst into tears, and Momma came into the room to see Papa
upset and angry and SweetPea still sobbing.

"What's going on here?" Dada cried.

"Our child is a thief!" Papa responded.

"What?" Momma was shocked.

"Yes, while we were at the bookstore today, SweetPea decided they were going to have a toy regardless of what we decided," Papa responded.

"Oh, SweetPea, how could you take something from the bookstore like that? Ms. Boatwright has always been so kind to you," Momma cried.

There are consequences for your actions, my child," said Papa. "Now get your coat and your stolen toy and get in the car – we're going back to the bookstore immediately! Mama, I know you want to go, but this is a lesson SweetPea needs to learn for their future, and I want to take SweetPea with me alone."

"Okay, sweetheart, I trust that you can handle this. sp looking back sadly
Besides, the baby's fussy and I don't want to take her.
I love you, and I'll see you when you get back," Momma said.

"I love you too, dear. We'll be back
soon," Papa said as they headed
outside and into the car.

SweetPea felt as though bricks were tied to their feet as they walked to the car. They kept wishing this was only a bad dream. Maybe Ms. Boatwright wouldn't be at the bookstore and then they would have to come another day. Maybe the car would get a flat tire and it would take so long to fix that the bookstore would close. Maybe they could magically reverse the day before they took the stolen toy. Maybe…

"We're here. It's time to face the consequences of your action today," Papa said.

SweetPea's heart pounded in their chest. Their hands began to sweat and they started to cry. "Papa, Papa, please, I'm so sorry! I know I was wrong, please don't make me tell Ms. Boatwright that I stole a toy from the bookstore!"

"My dear SweetPea, I love you more than words can say, and it hurts me to see you cry. But you are going to tell Ms. Boatwright that you stole a toy from her bookstore, and no amount of tears is going to change that," Papa explained. He kissed SweetPea on top of their head, and together, they walked into the bookstore to find Ms. Boatwright.

Time seemed to almost stop, passing so slowly that to SweetPea, the world started to move in slow motion.

"Can I help you?" the clerk said when they reached the counter.
"Yes, could you please tell Ms. Boatwright that Thomas Alexander and
SweetPea would like to talk to her in private if possible?" Papa said.
"Give me a moment to find her and I'll be right back,"
the clerk replied. A few moments later,
Ms. Boatwright began walking up the aisle toward them.

"Good afternoon, Mr. Alexander," she said. "How can I help you?"

"SweetPea has something they would like to say to you," Papa said.
Silence fell over the bookstore – in SweetPea's mind, all eyes were on them.

Papa quickly winked at her, indicating that she should not give
SweetPea any sympathy, and she understood. She was silent,
patiently waiting for SweetPea to talk.

"M-M-Ms. B-B-Boatwright,
I'm so sorry I took a toy
from your store today."

"SweetPea!" Papa warned quietly.

"I took… I mean, I stole a toy from your store today when I came to listen to Yami read. I know I was wrong b-b-but I…"

Ms. Boatwright interrupted. "Well, SweetPea, I have a policy that I follow when someone steals from my store."
She winked back at Papa.

"I call the police and have them take that person to jail for stealing. Stealing is against the law, and I won't tolerate anyone doing that in my store.
So I'm afraid I need to go and call the police now,"
she said.
She began to walk back toward her office.

SweetPea ran after her, pleading.

"Please, please, Ms. Boatwright, I'm very sorry!
You've always been kind to me,
I should never have taken anything from you and I never will again!"

"Hmm… is there something else SweetPea can do around the store to pay for the stolen toy?" Papa asked.

"I'm sorry, Mr. Alexander, that's not the store's policy," She replied.

"I'll do anything!" SweetPea begged.

"If you call the police, they'll take me to jail and I don't want to go to jail! I want to live with Momma and Papa and my baby sister, and to see my friends! I'm too small to play with tools! Papa said I can't use a hammer and break rocks! I'm supposed to be in school. They'll take me away from everything!" SweetPea cried.

"Did you ever think about all the things you could lose if you stole from me or anyone else? Did you think about not seeing your family or friends when you stole from me?" She asked.

"That was very careless of you. Your Momma and Papa and sister would miss you terribly, and they would have to come to jail just to visit you from behind a glass wall."

"No, I didn't think about all those things. I only thought about how much fun the toy was going to bring me," said SweetPea sadly.

"Well, did the toy bring you fun?" She asked.

"No, it didn't," said SweetPea.

"SweetPea, consider yourself very fortunate. I will not call the police, but you will have to work off the price of the toy in my shop. If that's okay with your Papa, of course," She said.

Papa hesitated and SweetPea started to cry. "That's very gracious of you, Ms. Boatwright, but SweetPea will have to work off double the price of the item," said Papa. "Then I think it will be fair."

"I'll work off triple if it keeps me out of jail and I can go home to my family!" SweetPea cried.

"Very well, triple it is. Is it okay if
SweetPea begins immediately?
I have some work they can start right
away if you have time today,
Mr. Alexander," She said.

"You are very kind to allow SweetPea to
work off the price of the toy instead of
calling the police," Papa said
before turning to SweetPea.
"Ms. Boatwright was kind enough to allow
you to work to cover the damages of the
stolen toy, but you are not allowed to keep
the toy even after you've worked for it. Is
that understood?"

SweetPea nodded quickly.
"Yes, Papa, I understand."

"Then, Ms. Boatwright, I will make time for SweetPea to work here in the bookstore. I just need to grab my laptop from my car. I'm fine waiting – I only need your Wi-Fi password, if that's okay. I have a project to complete for my work," said Papa.

Ms. Boatwright handed a piece of paper to Papa
with the password on it and then led SweetPea
to the storage room to begin work.
Several hours later, a very dusty but smiling SweetPea came walking
down the hallway of the bookstore toward Papa.

"Oh, Papa! You should see all the books and boxes of toys and magazines in the storage room! I helped to organize it all! It was so dusty in there, but I didn't mind. I'm just glad I get to go home with you to see my family!"

"Remember, you said triple the price," reminded Papa.

"I spoke to Momma and Ms. Boatwright, and we all agreed
that you would sweep and dust the children's area
during storytelling next time," Papa continued.
"Your friends might wonder why you're not sitting and
listening to the story, and then you will have to explain to them
why you're not participating."

SweetPea turned to Ms. Boatwright.

"I'm so sorry," they said softly.

"I should never have stolen.

Momma and Papa are disappointed in me, and I'm sad that I didn't

think about the consequences of my actions before I stole the toy."

When it came time for storytelling the next week, it was difficult for SweetPea to truly face the consequences of their actions. It was hard to explain to their friends why they couldn't participate.

SweetPea explained to
their friends that they did
something that needed to
be corrected.

They told their friends that they hadn't been kind
and had done a very selfish thing.
Now they were working to make things right.

BOOK STORE

At the end of storytelling time, just before SweetPea was about to leave with Momma and Papa, Ms. Boatwright came up to them. "SweetPea, you did a good job helping me in the bookstore," she said, "and I overheard you explaining to your friends why you couldn't participate in storytelling time. I appreciate your willingness to make things right. When you're old enough to work properly, I will hire you to help me in my store."

Momma and Mama were so pleased with SweetPea that for a surprise, they bought SweetPea the very same toy they had stolen! SweetPea joyfully went home with Momma, Mama, and their sister until life brings it's new adventure.